A Deaf Rose Climbs from a Broken World

Raelyn Green

BookLeaf Publishing

India | USA | UK

Presentation by *BookLeaf Publishing*

Web: www.bookleafpub.com

E-mail: info@bookleafpub.com

ISBN: 9789358313055

First edition 2023

DEDICATION

Dedicated to the broken girl inside of me &
those who've been with me through out my life,
my friends & family.

Mom & Dad Green, Green Siblings

AMODA & AFODA

Dr. J. Smith, Mrs. Andi W., & Dr. C. Tennant.

Dr. J. Delkamiller, Mrs. J. Shannon, Mrs.
Kruse, Ms. K. Newton, etc.

Dorm Staff: Patty D., Donna S., Pat VS.,
Maureen B., Jodie B., & Mr. Cool, etc.

ACKNOWLEDGEMENT

Thank You to everyone who has encouraged me to do this. Geri K., Elizabeth Z., Renee F., Betty G., Linda O., Kiana J., Jennie W., Ruthie O., & my Family (Green's)
A Special Shout Out to Trudi Jane for her feedback & input!

PREFACE

Abuse & Trauma, from childhood to today, has caused a lot of pain and brokenness. It's still a journey towards Hope, love, self-discovery, forgiveness and freedom.
Trapped in the past, I turn to poetry & songs to get where I'm to go. I've written what essentially comes down to fighting the darkness to have a life that's worth the price of living.
Thanks for caring enough to read what I've expressed and if it helps someone, then my vulnerability was not in vain.

Floating Puzzles

Multiple puzzles float in the water, incomplete,
Pieces surface of a past full of defeat.
Jumbled words float by, all are important pieces
This picture I have, fits only one of these.

Flashing through fractured memories of old,
Anguish, laughter, pain, joy and fear unfold.
Falling tears of different means, fitting any scene
Which puzzle does it belong to, which can be
seen?

So many memories in many different phases,
Confusion and uncertainty in multiple places.
It's impossible to ever complete the puzzles,
empty memories leave the scenes muddled.

The brain's very clever, protecting your overall
sanity,
Sinking parts of your memories, the ones of
inhumanity.
You stand near the water, squinting into the
depths,
Trying to see it all, perhaps it's best to not
intercept.

The Slate of The Girl Within

I'm tapped out,
No playful pout,
No strength to shout,
My mind is riddled with doubt.
My fist are pounding,
I'm slowly drowning,
Always frowning,
Never clowning.
Feeling forsaken,
Never awakened,
Forever shaken,
Won't be taken.

My heart breaks,
My dream wakes,
My soul craves to live,
My mind needs to forgive.

Is this the only path life is about?
Is this to continue being our fate?
Let me, with all my might, scream it all out,
Heal the broken girl within & start a new slate.

Deafly Silence

Life was never easy for me growing up,
Dodging fists, slaps, rulers and getting cut up.
The disdain to my heritage in the heat of
summer,
The insults to my Deafness in the throes of
slumber.

Very little I did could calm the raging storms,
Sneaks from behind, fingers squeezing and
bruises formed.
Gasping struggles ensued, what did I do to suffer
this crime?
Was my name yelled as I passed out and awoke
one more time?

Vulnerability was forbidden to be displayed,
In the silence, my acting slayed.
To be responsible for your happiness- insane,
What a weight I unfairly carried, in my head
ingrained.

You made my Deafness the opposite of strength,
Who would believe me and not keep me at arms
length.

No one else would want me, you bought my
silence,
You missed something vital, for born within was
self-reliance.

The Road We Are On

You made a promise,
broke it and my trust,
Did you forget or hope,
it'd just fade into dust.
Am I not important enough,
for you to keep your word,
This remains an issue,
I can't move forward.

This was no minor problem,
my life changed forever,
I still suffer the aftermath,
alone & in the aether.
We don't talk anymore,
I miss it, I need it,
I don't want to lose anyone,
I'm being legit.

My heart squeezes when I think of the distance,
My mind scrambles to chip away the resistance.
We're drifting further & further apart,
Can anyone fix a broken, shattered heart?

How many more I'm sorry's do I have to say,

How much more time do we have to throw
away?
I can't keep doing this, the limits not the sky,
Is it possible to reconnect or do we say
Goodbye?

Comfortmare

Laying in bed,
she showed up by my side,
She hugged me to her,
as I started to cry.
Brown hair and eyes of love and compassion,
Gentle arms and words expressed in action.

I was in a battle,
of an endless, horrific nightmare,
The past haunts me in my dreams,
a nightly affair.
I tell her my story, she listens, watches and gives relief,
She tells me I'm okay, that I'm not alone, she believes.

The broken and scary parts inside,
are put on hold,
For this moment, she fights for me,
a heart of Gold.
She's fought for women like me, she's a sight to see,
She invades my dreams, she becomes Deaf like me.

Though it's a nightmare,
she is real, just and true,
She lives and breathes,
has her own dreams too.
In the midst of my most invasive nightmares,
She conjures and renews in my mind- a
comfortmare.

Words Hurt

Her words and ridicule discouraged my heart,
She planted a seed that's insidious and dark.
Paving the way for resentment, anger and hate,
I tried so hard to not let it come to pass, too late.

I don't know why I trusted and put up with her,
She's hurt me so many times, it's a blur.
It seems I draw people that hurt me the most,
The same old song- giving up the ghost.

One particular night, forever etched in my mind,
Her screams loud and dehumanizing.
So many people could hear what she said,
Saw me run out with tears, they hugged me
instead.

She's not a part of my life anymore,
I finally had the courage to close that door.
She can't hurt me, though her words remain,
Another scar inside I should not have gained.

Words Unheard

Pictures are all we have left,
Memories in time is all we get.
To see you face to face is denied,
Emotions caught in pieces at a time.

There's not enough time in a day,
Many words, thought and things I need to say.
Too often they're ignored and spurned,
Suppressed so deeply it burns.

My heart and soul were broken,
Sometimes they're even frozen.
It may still be beating though it's dead,
The same old thing everyday I dread.

Not many memories newly made,
Not many people in my life stayed.
What was my life ever worthy for,
Rejection invades my deepest core.

Triggered

So many hidden Triggers
Of course it's such a Kicker
An Outpouring of Emotions
Going through the Motions

You'd think I'd have it handled
It's actually a conflicting scandal
Always falling short of expectations
It's a wonder I'm not under sedation

A life in isolated dissatisfaction
Scrambling to regain total traction
Approval and acceptance vie for attention
When life is full of disdainful apprehension

To control a triggers eventful acceleration
Helped by calm supportive considerations
Instead are fed by others negative reactions
Triggered emotions thus result in overreactions

Too Much To Lose

Left standing in the silence of your departure,
I broke, changed and was draped in silence.
The elements ebbing and flowing, hit harsher,
My heart hardened in the darkness, defiant.

Angry, betrayed, aggrieved and shattered,
Watching as the lights disappear from sight.
I'll never return, a vow, not that it mattered,
I was at fault, the reason for much pain that
night.

Everything changed, new emotions brewed,
Envy, resentment, disappointment and distrust.
Apologies meant nothing, actions misconstrued,
I can't bear to lose them, I'd rather turn to dust.

The child within struggles, the adult you see
does too,
Left behind to fight alone, to survive and go on.
Then I knew to never again give my heart, to
pursue,
For I've already once trusted and now it's gone.

Eternally Flamed Fear

I Fear I will fall sleep one day and not awaken,
Finding myself in the abyss or in the fires of
hell.
Perhaps from an overdose or intense heartbreak,
Easily forgotten in death, as in life, with no
farewell.

You all forget- I think differently and am easily
bored,
Thinking I know better and should do what you
say.
I'm tired of being preached at & constantly
ignored,
That alone does more damage and turns me
away.

Your actions confuse me, as do your conflicting
words,
I can't follow the logic nor figure out what they
mean.
I've tried, I always fail and flail, backwards &
forewords,
I can't do better without patience, practice and
scenes.

I'm afraid that the Heaven I envision, will be
true,
Just recently my view was asked- uncommonly
casted.
It's not paradise, though no negative memories
brew,
Those you don't want to see & those in Hell-
Erased.

Either way- we're still separated eternally.

The Domino Effect

You lied and manipulated me from the start,
You stabbed me in the back- in the dark.
You set up a grand stage, creating your lie,
You didn't care who you trampled- you're sly.

I learned the truth years later, it was too late,
I was dealt a bad hand, an insufferable fate.
Should of known you'd take such lengths,
Anticipating your strategies wasn't my strength.

Little did I know, my hope was within reach,
Two parties wanting to be together- cheated.
Snatched away with crafty & cunning deceit,
A future uncertain & relationships breeched.

The mountain I climbed, started with rocks,
I slipped & fell onto treacherous blocks.
There's no way to fix the disaster you caused,
I just need to win the battle I could've fought.

Universal Roles

Emotions whizzing past my mind & eyes,
Oceans of tears I furiously swipe & despise.
My pulse races fast & aids me to roar high,
Dropped my head, expelling a weary sigh.

A thousand sentences slide, rise & ebbs,
Which one to pull & voice to lure into a web.
Loneliness breeds a sad tale as old as time,
Sharing souls span across universal lines.

Dawn begins a new light, traveling the skies,
Searching to shine upon a soul wanting to die.
As the last of the nights darkness fades away,
Time has never been so precious as that day.

Fires rage across the earth, volcanoes burst,
Wind and Rain swirl & dance totally rehearsed,
Combining elements to bring precious cargo,
A soulful clash, lightning flashing- a beautiful
glow.

Autumns Changes

It's getting colder, there'll soon be Autumn
Leaves,
Changing from Green to Red, Orange & Gold.
As the Sun Rises and sets, it spreads with ease,
Views of everything golden- a sight to behold.

Not all will appreciate it as the months roll by,
Everything evolves with the passing of time.
Capture what you can for todays end is surely
nigh,
Tomorrow isn't promised, caste a vision in your
mind.

No season is the same, though its repeated in
order,
Even then, the order can bring false hope, just
like life.
Spring, Summer, Fall and Winter, like a broken
recorder,
Yet one day it's Summer, then Winter & Spring-
what strife!

Just remember, each True season has beauty all
its own,

You can't change what you view as they come
and they go.
There's always beauty at the beginning, it's set
in stone,
Autumns glow is here, take a picture, for
nothing stays Gold.

Incurable Power of Pain

Laying down, tears streaming,
Curled in a ball, I'm screaming.
The pain, stabbing knives and barbwire,
Lightning, electric wires around all sides.

My mind is chaotic, sifting through the pain,
My body jerks as it rides through each strain.
Medication, ice, heat pads do nothing for it,
How do I control pain at this level without a fit?

It consumes me, I can't get out of bed easily,
It spreads everywhere & my lungs labor
wheezily.
I wish I could reach inside and pull it all out,
That'd be a gory sight & unwise without a
doubt.

There's no cure, will I ever get to live without
pain,
Will I ever get used to it or will it drive me
insane.
Wondering if this time will be worse than the
last,
It'd be nice to someday say, that's all in the past.

The Soul's Lyrics in Songs

How many songs have I listened to wistfully,
The lyrics are amazing but I can't relate to them.
I'm just a girl, with a past that failed dismally,
Those songs were written for the lucky gems.

It's never easy when you know you're different,
How could it be, when fighting for everything is
the norm.
Like salmon swimming upstream, against the
current,
You can't help feel like, inside of you,
everything's torn.

You click with songs even when they aren't your
life's truth,
The soul's showing you what it loves, desires &
needs.
It isn't always realistic nor is it easily achieved,
such struth!
It emotes the good & bad within, but you won't
be eased.

Still, I listen, sometimes I cry & it's an act we
can call a win,

A song should touch your soul, whether it hurts
you or not.
They paint a picture of the person, of her soul,
deep within,
There's songs your soul aches for, your ultimate
thoughts

Secrets Chaos

There are secrets
everywhere you look & turn,
On the ground we stand,
in the air we breathe.
They're in the rise & setting of the sun that
burns,
They're told to us, hidden within & causing
unease.

Secrets can make or break us,
it can't be undone,
Designed to place fear
deep within our heart.
It can't be changed,
thus falling apart will or has begun,
Though some try to channel it,
hide it within our art.

We craft masks of subterfuge,
keeping you in the dark,
Pain and Fear,
covered by the masks of illusion.
We don't initiate first,
afraid you'll see into our hearts,
The illusion I wear protects you

I remain elusive.

Whispering a secret in another's ear,
it carry's in the air,
If you're not careful,
it can reach someone perverse,
Renewing the secrets cycle and chaotic despair,
We were better off not knowing, for a secret can
be cursed.

Crafting Life

Standing in the pouring rain,
Tears streaming down my face.
Left behind with hopes in vain,
No place to go except through this place.

Little Girl inside, there's more to come,
If the rain can stop, the sun will come out,
Don't close your eyes til the last chord is done,
Release your doubts, sing the song out loud.

Live to fight another day, to leave this phase,
Weary heads held high with a heavy crown,
Eyes face the sky, etched with a teary gaze,
The trials & pain we face, force us to the
ground.

Left wondering why we experience this fate,
As we stand in the rain and hope they look back,
Once again, tears flow down & the heart breaks,
This life will be hard & it's now ours to artfully
craft.

Ghosting Damage

Nothing stays the same, so much has changed,
Time has flown, people move on and I'm
estranged.
No safety net in sight has been my life for years,
No one can count the tears I've shed and
cleared.

Some things can't heal, like loved ones ghosting
me,
Ghosting is abandonment, best to give upfront
decrees.
You're writing me off, leaving me, chipping off
my heart,
Emotions get mangled, trust is skewed from the
start.

Did you know it's damaging? It's insanely hard
to erase,
You shatter the respect you had, it's not a good
face.
If I did something first, two wrongs don't make
a right,
You've no idea the impact, your image drops
from sight.

You struck the heart, gambled souls and changed
mindsets,
Out of sync stepping stones cause future failed
tests.
You may not understand the good image you had
at one time,
If faced with this again, remember, emotions
don't stop on a dime.

Living with Light & Dark

There's light and darkness
everywhere you look,
It swirls around you, inside you,
can you feel it?
It's in the depths of your soul,
find their hooks,
You're caught in a battle,
which will you let win?

They beckon, entice
caress your heart & mind,
Seeking to be familiarized,
to suppress its enemy.
Both are comforting,
in one you may briefly hide,
True darkness leaves no room for light,
its envied.

Darkness becomes tedious,
light now craved,
It's a battle you started,
only you can choose.
Tangible surroundings
the easiest craze,
It's the intangible

that gives life its truest truth.

Darkness cannot exist with light
Nor can Death exist with life
Turn them around & the opposite is true…
For Light can exist with Darkness
Alas, Life can with Death in all its harshness.

The Long Road

The tunnel is long & dark
It fills me with dread
I can't calm my beating heart
There's a light up ahead

Running isn't getting me closer
No one is around to hear me shout
The air rushes around, it's colder
I'm overwhelmed and time is running out

Tears Flowing
Heart Exposed
Razor Bloody Scars.
An Aching Hunger
for a loving stroke
Be Empowered
Touch the Stars

Facing Obstacles
Push the Fear away
Feeling Lonely in the Night
Often led astray
Watch the Sun & the Moon
They're your Guiding Light

Dare to Dance
Live Life Freely
Take a Chance
Chase Your Dreams

Lullaby

Goodbye
Don't cry
This is my last lullaby
Wipe those tears from your eyes.

I'm damaged goods
I never belonged
My heart changed
my pain's now stone.
The weight I carried
for far too long
Burned me inside out
suffering alone.

Eyes shifted from me
backs turned away
I wanted to go home
the way was blocked.
What-ifs abound
Now invalid plays
Scenarios imagined
revealed decocted.

I'll rise up again
fly straight into the night

The wind in my hair
I'm gonna be free.
Towards the Stars
I'll fly to the light
No longer tied
No more forces I can't see